RISE OF THE ROBOTS!

ROBOTS ENFORCING THE LAW

WILL ROBOTS TAKE OVER THE WORLD?

Louise Spilsbury

CHERITON
CHILDREN'S BOOKS

Published in 2024 by **Cheriton Children's Books**
1 Bank Drive West, Shrewsbury, Shropshire, SY3 9DJ, UK

First Edition

Author: Louise Spilsbury
Designer: Paul Myerscough
Editor: Jennifer Sanderson
Proofreader: Katie Dicker

Picture credits: Cover: Shutterstock/Evgeniyqw (top), Shutterstock/Digital Storm (left), Shutterstock/Gorodenkoff (right). Inside: p1: Shutterstock/Digital Storm, p4: Shutterstock/Robert P Alvarez, p5: Shutterstock/Tsuneomp, pp6-7: Shutterstock/Hacohob, p6: Shutterstock/Alice-photo, p7: Shutterstock/Lev Radin, p8: Shutterstock/Kandl Stock, p9: Shutterstock/Neglected Frames, p10: OTSAW, p11: Shutterstock/Evgeniyqw/Artem Varnitsin, p12: Smart City Expo/Sparta Digital, p13: Shutterstock/Sarah Holmlund, p14: Shutterstock/Pressmaster, p15b: Wikimedia Commons/Robobotics, p15t: Shutterstock/Glynnis Jones, p16: Shutterstock/SpiritProd33, p17: Shutterstock/Varavin88, p18: Shutterstock/Jai Agnish, p19: Shutterstock/AstroVictor, p20: Shutterstock/Frame Stock Footage, p21b: Wikimedia Commons/Do-Rishiony Tel Aviv, p21t: Shutterstock/Hasan Akbas, p22b: Shutterstock/Mgr Nobody, p22t: Wikimedia Commons/NASA, p23: Stanford University/École Polytechnique Fédérale de Lausanne, p24: Avy, p25b: Shutterstock/Frenzel, p25t: Avy, p26: Shutterstock/R R, p27: Shutterstock/Alexander Oganezov, p28: Shutterstock/Digital Storm, p29b: Shutterstock/Leolintang, p29r: ICOR Technology, p30: Shutterstock/Cast Of Thousands, p31tl: Alamy/Associated Press, p31tr: Shutterstock/Ziga Cetrtic, p32: Alamy/Robert Harding, p33: Shutterstock/Davizro Photography, p34: Alamy/Sipa US, p35: Shutterstock/IZF, pp36-37: Shutterstock/Gorodenkoff, p37: Shutterstock/Frame Stock Footage/Asharkyu, p38: Shutterstock/Andrei Kobylko, p39l: Shutterstock/Golfx, p39r: Adobestock/Zilvergolf, pp40-41: Shutterstock/Jaz Online, p41: General Robotics, p42: Shutterstock/Evren Kalinbacak, p43: Howe and Howe Inc, p44: Adobestock/Maren Winter, p45: Adobestock/Sushiman.

Printed in China

CONTENTS

Chapter 1

PATROLLING THE STREETS

It's the dead of night. A police siren wails in the distance. You hear the sound of trashcans being knocked over and glass being broken. Rumors spread about a protest that's turned violent. Law enforcement is stretched. There never seem to be enough police officers to go around or to patrol all of the streets. What if there was something that could make every neighborhood in the world safer, even the most dangerous places where most people never dare to go?

A NEW TYPE OF COP

Robots are the newest members of law enforcement forces around the world. These moving machines can be programmed to tackle many police tasks. They can help patrol streets at night, stop criminals carrying weapons, chase robbers escaping a crime scene in a stolen automobile, and can help in **hostage** situations. Robots can be fitted with different types of equipment too. For example, they have cameras for **surveillance** to watch possible criminal activity, heavy-lifting gear to clear large obstacles, and devices to **defuse** bombs so they don't explode.

Robotic police will put themselves in the line of fire so human police officers won't have to.

ROBOTS OR PEOPLE?

Being a law enforcement officer is risky. Officers put themselves in harm's way every day to protect others. Using robots makes life less dangerous for human officers. For example, in 2019, a man had tried to set fire to a gas station and was thought to be carrying a gun. Officers sent in a robot to give the man a cell phone so an officer at a safe distance away could talk to him. Robots can also do an officer's ordinary and sometimes-boring tasks without getting tired or losing their focus on the job.

Could robots be the future of the world's police forces?

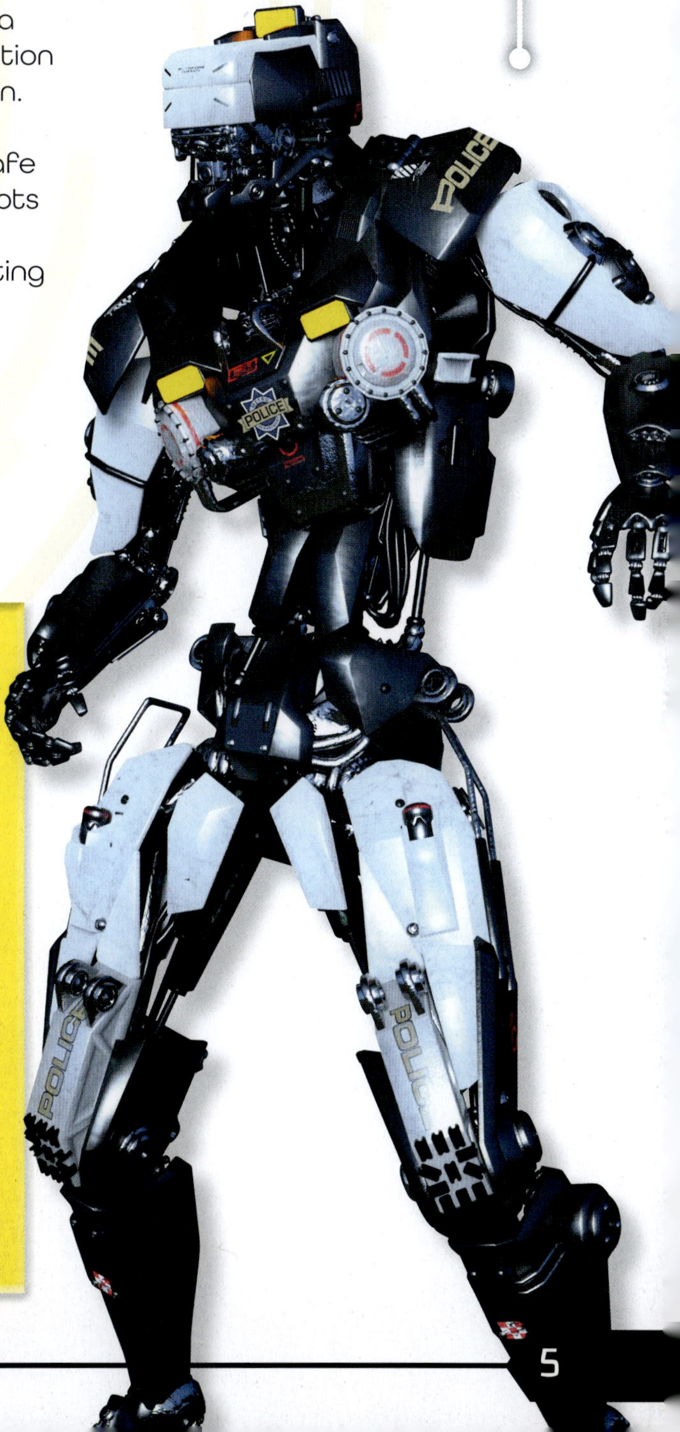

BIG BOT DEBATE

Is Replacing Human Officers with Robots a Good or Bad Idea?

Some people say robotic cops are a great idea. They argue that if something goes wrong during an operation, damage to or loss of a robot is far better than injury to or death of a human police officer. Others disagree. They say that at the moment, people program and control robotic cops. However, if robots began to operate without humans they might act dangerously. Do you think robotic officers would be an advantage or disadvantage?

Police use surveillance and security cameras to prevent and detect crime.

ALWAYS ON THE BEAT

Police officers are regularly in high-speed car chases with dangerous criminals. True or false? False! There may be some exciting and tense moments but most police work is the same every day, takes a lot of time, and many would say, is quite boring. Switch on a law enforcement robot, and the bot is on-task. It will just carry on doing whatever it is programmed to do, no matter what the job is.

UNDER CONTROL

To be useful, law enforcement robots need to be very easy and convenient to control. They need to be able to use tools that can help them achieve their mission. Most robots are controlled by operators, who give commands for the moving parts of the robot to follow. This is done via the movements of a **joystick** or other hand controller.

ROBOT SENSES

Robots can also control themselves. They have a range of **sensors** that allow them to see, smell, hear, and touch. Robots have extra abilities, too. For example, some robots have LiDAR systems. These bounce **laser** beams off surrounding objects to figure out how far away things are. LiDAR helps the robots move around without bumping into things.

SECURITY BOTS

Criminals are always on the lookout for places to target, for example, a quiet ATM, an empty property, or the place where goods are loaded onto trucks, ships, or trains. Security guards often work at these places but it can be difficult for them to remain watchful all the time or to be in the right place at the right time to catch a criminal. This is where high-tech security robots can be very useful.

ROBOTS RISING UP!

Patrolling empty warehouses and malls is necessary work but it can be dull. Not for the Knightscope K3! The K3 is a fully autonomous wheeled bot. This means it does not need humans to control it. As it roams the corridors, its sensors look for anything out of place.

SPOTTING CRIMINALS

Advanced security robots such as the Knightscope K1 Hemisphere help keep places safe and secure. Attached to a wall at eye level, this bot's cameras provide **high-definition** video. Its computer system links to a **database** for **facial recognition** and automatic license plate recognition. Identifying the criminal and their getaway vehicle is made simple!

The Knightscope K3 keeps going without help by plugging in itself when its battery needs recharging.

NEIGHBORHOOD WATCH

In the still of the night, some areas use neighborhood watch programs to keep people safe. Residents keep a lookout for anything that seems out of place. But, in other neighborhoods, they use robots. They are the smart eyes and ears of security. They are there to offer help and comfort if things go wrong. These bots work alongside police officers to increase the security presence in an area so people feel safer.

PARK PATROLLER

It's not just the houses the bots watch over. The Knightscope K5 that patrols a Los Angeles park has POLICE written on its egg-shaped body. It is about 5 feet (1.5 m) tall and wheels along at about 3 miles per hour (4.8 kph). This robot's video cameras monitor what it sees 24/7. Its microphones are programmed to listen out for unusual sounds. If K5's computer detects that something is wrong, such as a person acting suspiciously, it can send footage directly to officers' phones. This alerts the officers, who can then go to the scene to find out what is going on, and possibly make an arrest and solve a crime.

This orange-and-black traffic control robot is on patrol in Changi Airport, Singapore.

In China, robotic police assist human officers on the streets.

ON THE LOOKOUT

In Singapore, specialist robotic cops have been handing out justice. Their target is anyone who behaves in a way that might affect others. Xavier is a small four-wheeler with sensors for autonomous **navigation** and cameras to spot trouble.

BAD BEHAVIOR

Xavier is programmed to spot offenses, or crimes, such as smoking in **prohibited** areas, the illegal selling of goods, and bicycles parked in non-approved places. Xavier then sends an alert to the police command and control center, so officers can attend if necessary. It gives warnings to stop such behavior and displays messages to educate the public about what they are and are not allowed to do.

ROBOTS RISING UP!

Patrol robots don't always get it right. One K5 fell in a fountain and another accidentally struck a toddler at a shopping mall. During the Covid-19 pandemic when there were strict social distancing rules in place, a Xavier robot stopped in front of a group of people watching chess and warned "Please keep 1-meter distancing, please keep to 5 persons per group!"

Autonomous security robot O-R3 can patrol outdoors all day and all night.

CRUISING THE CITY

For anyone walking home at night, the steady blue and red lights of a police patrol car can be reassuring because they know someone is watching out for them. In parts of some cities, robotic patrol cars are on duty, helping keep the streets safe.

POCKET-SIZED PATROL CAR

The O-R3 is far too small to carry a driver, but it doesn't need one. O-R3 has all-round video camera vision and a sophisticated onboard computer to help it patrol. The robot learns its patrol routes. The computer builds a map of O-R3's surroundings using LiDAR. This locates and measures features in the nearby environment. O-R3 then figures out its position within the area.

SPOTTING SUSPECTS

The O-R3 has a thermal camera, which picks up heat from living things, so it can help officers see in the dark and when they can't get inside a building. Facial-recognition software checks out the faces of people it passes and compares them to a database of wanted criminals. If there is a match, officers are called from the control center to make an arrest.

OWN GOAL

Goalie II is an urban patrol robot used in South Korea. It is a bit like a bumper car and it navigates autonomously through city areas. It has two LiDAR systems to spot and avoid obstacles or things in the way, while following **GPS**-programmed routes. Goalie II's cameras can see in daylight or darkness to keep an eye on high-crime areas. This is especially useful in areas that have police camera blind spots. These are places that street cameras don't see, and so are areas in which criminal activity might take place.

ROBOTS RISING UP!

Robot pairs can help keep the streets safe together, just like the human cop partners in a regular patrol car. If O-R3 spots a suspect, it can flip open its hood to release a drone. This flying robot can rise and use its cameras to keep track of the suspect from the air, at up to 300 feet (91 m) high. The police can keep observing with the drone even if O-R3 is too slow to follow or if the suspect escapes the streets.

Drones are able to easily track people on the move anywhere, day and night.

ROBOT TAKEOVER: REAL-LIFE ROBOCOP

How would you feel if you were walking along your street and then spotted a robot dressed as a law enforcement officer on the beat? People in Dubai in the United Arab Emirates (UAE) are getting used to this, because this is where the world's first Robocop is on patrol.

Robot Lieutenant

Robocop has a star on its shoulder strap, meaning that it is a Lieutenant in the Dubai Police. It is about 5 feet (1.5 m) tall and weighs a little more than an average man. Robocop is programmed to speak in English and Arabic but soon will be able to speak Russian, Chinese, French, and Spanish.

Just a Friendly Neighborhood Cop

Robocop has cameras for eyes, and its computer can identify not only people's emotions and facial expressions but also their hand gestures. This means it can figure out when someone is sad or happy or frowning or smiling. It can then react in the right way to help people by understanding what they want and what they are feeling.

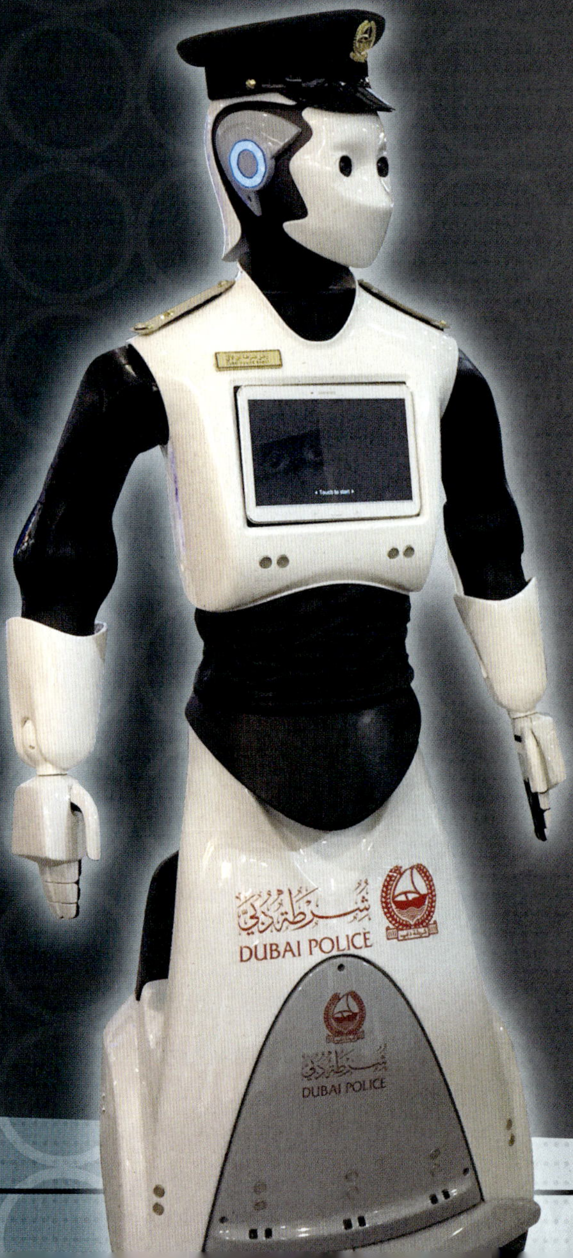

Robocop interacts with people like a human cop. It can even shake hands and salute!

Could robotic police officers of the future patrol our streets, armed and ready to defend us?

On the Spot

If a thief snatches a bag in a mall or tourist area, Robocop is on hand to help. People can talk to it or tap a touchscreen on the robot's chest to report the crime right there at the crime scene—they don't need to go to a police station. Robocop's cameras can feed live video of the crime scene or ongoing criminal activity to the police control center. Then, officers take action based on what they see. Robocop is also an expert at facial recognition so it can recognize the offender itself.

BIG BOT DEBATE

Are Robocops the Future or Should They Be Left in the Present?

Some people say that Robocops are the future of street patrolling because robots can patrol 24/7 so officers can get on with more immediate tasks. Other people are not so sure. They argue that the Robocop could malfunction, or stop working properly, and then wrongly identify a criminal or criminal behavior. Then police officers would have to waste time responding to and fixing the mistake. Do you think Robocops could help or do you believe they are a hazard?

Chapter 2

STAKEOUT!

Before the police can make an arrest, they need to gather evidence that proves that the suspect is guilty. And when they are about to make an arrest, they need to know other potentially life-saving information. Knowing if a suspect is carrying a weapon or if other criminals are hiding nearby, waiting to ambush the police, can be the difference between life and death. This type of surveillance is a very important part of law enforcement.

SECRET PATROLS

Some surveillance operations involve watching or patrolling an area for a long time. It can take a while for criminals to appear, and this is when robots can help. Unmanned ground vehicles (UGVs) can be used for surveillance.

Small, with four wheels or caterpillar treads, UGVs are designed to travel under obstacles and over uneven surfaces without toppling over. They can operate without human control. They follow preprogrammed routes by using GPS. Because these UGVs are small, they can spy on criminals from small spaces. Using UGVs prevents putting human police officers in the line of fire.

UGVs could record criminal activity without being noticed.

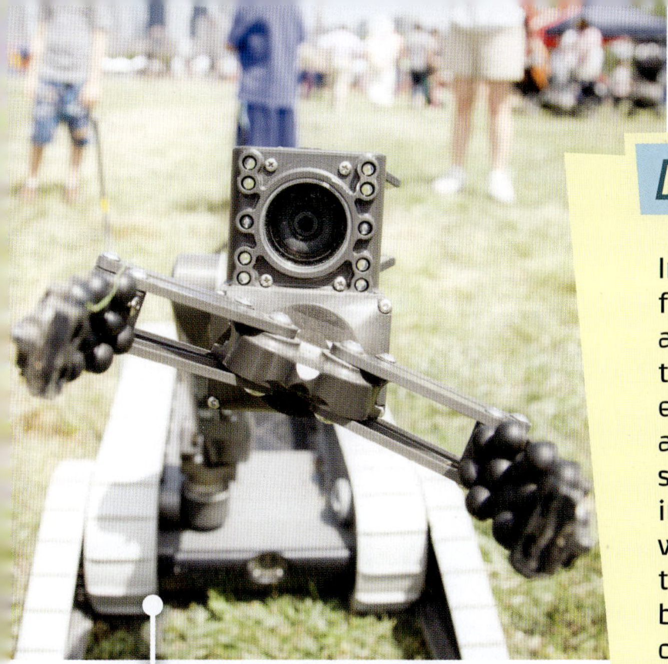

UGVs are used to locate and **dispose** of explosive devices, such as bombs, which helps keep human officers safe.

ROBOTS RISING UP!

In 2013, the person responsible for exploding a bomb during the annual Boston Marathon managed to escape the police. Then law enforcement received word that a local man had spotted a blood-soaked person hiding beneath a tarp in a boat. Officers sent a helicopter with a thermal camera to the scene to confirm that there was a live body under the tarp. Then, more officers gathered at the scene. Before making the arrest, they sent in a robot to pull off the tarp and to check that the suspect was not still armed with explosives.

SEEING BEHIND CLOSED DOORS

What if police officers have **intelligence** that a group is planning a serious crime or an act of **terrorism** but the criminals are in hiding? Enter IRIS, which stands for Individual Robotic Intelligence System. It is a small UGV that can motor into confined spaces, above or underground, to gather information. This tough little robot can be thrown over high walls to enable police to view a situation in **real time**. It can drive over uneven surfaces and is controlled by a tablet computer to allow operators to explore dangerous locations from a safe distance away.

IRIS is also being used by the armed forces to gather intelligence about enemies.

EYES IN THE SKIES

It can take several police officers and many police helicopters and cars to track or chase criminals and their vehicles. But, surveillance drones can cover a lot of ground quickly and as they fly in the air, suspects are less likely to see them.

BRING ON THE DRONES!

Drones are small and compact, and so fit easily in the trunk of a police vehicle. Law enforcement officers can have them in the air in minutes to help them monitor and capture video footage and images of an incident. The drones can be flown over an area to follow suspects and monitor their activities. Drones can also easily drop down and land.

From this vantage point, their cameras can aim at an area, filming hours of video footage while staying safely out of sight.

A DAY AND NIGHT WATCH

Police drones can survey, or study, an area at night just as well as they can during daylight. As well as an onboard camera, drones have thermal imaging technology. This senses heat given off by the human body and can help officers locate people in the dark or who may be hiding among bushes or trees. Once officers know where the suspects are, they can find and arrest them.

Police drones can cover a large area in a short amount of time and flush out suspects on the ground.

ROBOTS RISING UP!

Large numbers of drones working together are known as a swarm. Swarm unmanned aerial vehicles (UAVs) can fly autonomously without an operator controlling them or one operator can control many drones at the same time. Together, a swarm of drones will be able to follow a suspect, even if they are running through crowded streets. Once the suspect is identified, the drones can avoid all obstacles, from other people to street furniture such a lampposts. The UAVs can even predict a suspect's route based on programmed maps. Then different drones in the swarm can get ahead, to the sides, above, and behind the suspect. There is no escape!

Criminals trying to get away under the cover of darkness can be tracked and chased by swarms of drones in the sky.

BORN TO FLY

Most law enforcement UAVs are multicopters—they usually have four spinning **propellers** or sets of two blades, and can hover, or stay still, in the air. The propellers or blades are fixed onto a frame that also holds a battery and any camera and other sensors.

Shock-absorbing feet allow the drone to land gently. Police on the ground use a handset to control the propellers that are operated by battery-powered motors. UAVs have built-in computers called flight controllers, too. These can adjust the motor speed automatically to steady the drone if a sudden gust of wind knocks it off course.

ROBOT TAKEOVER:

SMART AERIAL MONITORING

The Super Bowl is a world-famous sporting event that takes place each year. Law enforcement officers consider it to be a target for thieves, terrorists, and other criminals. Several thousand police officers are involved in monitoring the game and the events leading up to it. They plan and run practice drills for months beforehand. The streets are blocked off and uniformed and plainclothes police officers patrol the stadium to ensure safety. In 2020 other members of the police squad were on duty too: the Smart Aerial Monitoring System (SAMS-T) drones.

Super Bowl Security

The SAMS-T is a tethered drone system. A tether is a power line that allows a drone to fly for several hours without the need for it to stop, return to base, and recharge its batteries. That means it can keep constant watch. It can operate at up to 300 feet (91 m) and provides live video images of a wide area. Another big advantage is that because SAMS-T is a tethered drone, it can follow a suspect continuously, without having to pass from a fixed camera to another, and risk a delay, which could mean that a suspect is lost in a large crowd of people.

The Super Bowl is a challenge for law enforcement officers. More than 70,000 people gather inside and outside the stadium.

Small, flying drones are ideally designed for surveillance work at events with large crowds.

Successful Security

At the 2020 Super Bowl, the SAMS-T drones provided immediate and important information to police on the ground. Continual video streams were sent directly to a real-time crime center. That meant the police were able to spot incidents and deploy, or send out, officers to intervene or provide assistance where necessary.

Free Flying

SAMS is another drone in the monitoring system. It's a lightweight **quadcopter** that can stay in the air for around 50 minutes. It can be operated remotely and returns to a ground station to recharge. It can take off, fly, and land autonomously, even from a moving vehicle. The drone can also be programmed to take off automatically when triggered by a security alarm, such as a fence alarm or a distress call.

BIG BOT DEBATE

Is UAV Surveillance Useful or Just an Invasion of Privacy?

Law enforcement relies on human stakeouts to keep an eye on criminal activities. Some people think that using robots to watch people is going to be vital in helping police investigate and survey suspects. Other people have concerns that robots keeping a watchful eye 24/7 could invade innocent people's privacy. Do you think having robotic surveillance is a good or bad thing?

Chapter 3

SEARCH AND RESCUE

Police search-and-rescue teams play a vital part in finding lost and missing people. Some people go missing because they are confused and get lost but others may be missing because they have been kidnapped, or taken against their will. Some police robots are designed to help officers find and rescue victims, especially from dangerous situations.

BOTS TO THE RESCUE

Using robots to find and rescue people has several advantages. Sometimes the person in trouble may be in a building that is badly damaged, for example, after a bomb explosion, making it unsafe to enter. Or perhaps the person who needs to be rescued is surrounded by criminals who are ready to fire weapons if police officers approach. Search-and-rescue robots can locate and help the person in danger, without getting hurt.

Hostage situations can be dangerous for the people being held and for the law enforcement officers trying to rescue them.

HOSTAGE SITUATIONS

When someone is being held hostage, robots can be remotely controlled to deliver phones and supplies to the kidnapper. This allows the police to talk to and negotiate with the kidnapper. Some robots can sneak into buildings if the suspects have barricaded themselves in, to find out what weapons the criminals have and how many there are.

BREAKING AND ENTERING?

When the little bots have done their jobs, automated bulldozers can be directed to clear obstacles. If someone needs rescuing from a building where a wall has collapsed, for example, these robots can help clear a path so police officers can enter the building. These big bots have a robotic arm with metal blades at the end that can tear, crush, drag, and lift vehicles or smash bricks, metal, and wood. They can be fitted with gripping arms to move **debris**. They can break through doors, gates, barriers, and walls to allow officers to get inside.

ROBOTS RISING UP!

In the future, as well as keeping police officers safe by entering dangerous situations in their place, robots are likely to carry out more police rescue work. For example, hostage situations can get out of hand quickly and police, criminals, and the victims can be hurt. If a robot is sent into a hostage situation instead of a person, the robot can reduce the threat without shooting the criminal, for example, by releasing a sleeping gas.

Robotic bulldozers can clear a path through barricades or debris so that police officers can carry out rescues.

INSPIRED BY NATURE

Before a police officer can rescue someone, they need to know exactly where they are. Although humans and highly trained dogs will always be important in search-and-rescue operations, many new robots are being used as the eyes and ears in dangerous situations, to help find victims. Drones can be used to locate people but they can struggle to fly in small spaces and can't carry much. Land robots cannot cope with stairs, rubble, and closed doors. Designers have taken inspiration from the natural world to create robots that can deal with these challenges.

Snakebots are so agile they can climb up and around challenging spaces.

SNAKEBOTS IN ACTION

The long body of a robotic snake, or snakebot, is made up of many different sections. This allows it to bend and twist in different directions and into different shapes. Rubber grippers on the underside help it grip and slither through rubble, tiny holes, or narrow spaces such as pipes. Snakebots are battery powered and controlled by a remote-control joystick. They have lights and a camera to help operators see a real-time view. Snakebots also have a two-way microphone and speaker, so the operator can talk to victims to reassure them and also get information about what medical assistance they need.

ROBO-WASPS

Researchers have developed small drones that are about as heavy as a bar of soap but can move objects 40 times their own weight. FlyCroTugs were inspired by wasps, which can drag food too heavy for them to lift across the ground. FlyCroTug can fly through very small spaces but it can also stay on land and use grippers and tiny metal hooks to hold onto objects. It also has a powerful tether to pull the objects out of the way.

FLYCROTUGS

FlyCroTugs can work together to grab a door handle and tug a door open. That means they can open a door to get access to hostages or people who are trapped. They can drag objects that weigh much more than they do, such as cameras and water bottles, which can be useful in rescue situations. In the future, FlyCroTugs could potentially move pieces of debris or position a camera to help police monitor a dangerous situation.

ROBOTS RISING UP!

FlyCroTugs also took inspiration from gecko and insect feet. To grip smooth surfaces, the robots have a non-sticky **adhesive** that mimics, or copies, a gecko's intricate toe structures. For rough surfaces, they have 32 fish-hook-like metal spikes that can individually latch onto small pits in a surface.

FlyCroTugs are flying, micro, tugging robots!

ROBOT TAKEOVER: DRONE PLANE

Imagine a major emergency situation, such as a terror attack, which affects a large part of a city. There is widespread panic and a lot of people need assistance urgently. As well as law enforcement officers, other first responders are called to the scene, such as firefighters, medics, and bomb squad units. How do the police, and other emergency services, know where to start and where to go? This is where the latest drones, such as Aera, take control of the skies.

First Responder

Drones like Aera can be instantly sent into the air from a nearby **docking station**. They can arrive at the scene before first responders. They send real-time images of the emergency that show police and the different forces where they need to go and what to do first. Real-time video footage from drones helps chiefs to figure out which and how many units will be needed in the situation. It helps them decide how each unit can be used best to keep the public, emergency workers, and other first responders safe. This type of coordinated response saves lives.

Aera even has a temperature-controlled compartment for the safe delivery of medicines in a medical emergency.

Aera drones can keep a safe distance above flames while assessing the fire for the firefighters who have to deal with it.

Aera in Action

Aera is an unusual drone. It is a **fixed-wing** drone and like a drone plane, it can fly far, for a long time. But it is also very nimble, and can take off and land vertically like a helicopter. Aera flies autonomously and it can be fitted with a camera with zoom capability to see activity on the ground in detail. It also has a thermal camera to see in dim light or through smoke and flames. In case of fire, the Aera drone can be instantly sent to fly over the area where the flames are most ferocious. Firefighters on the ground can monitor the fire on the heat camera's live feed, so they can tackle the blaze safely.

BIG BOT DEBATE

Are Aerial Drones Effective in an Emergency?

Some people say drones are a very effective addition to any emergency service. They can often reach people in need more quickly than air or ground vehicles. They can assess situations or prevent accidents in risk-prone zones. Others argue that relying on these drones is a risk. Such technology is no substitution for human first responders. Do you think aerial drones are helpful or could they make emergency situations more difficult to deal with?

Chapter 4

BOMB DISPOSAL

When people spot a suspicious-looking package, they should call the police to remove it in case it is a bomb. Bombs can cause life-threatening and life-altering injuries. Detecting, **disarming**, and disposing of explosive devices is the risky job police bomb squads face. When robotic bomb disposal units take over this dangerous work, human officers are much safer.

DETECT THE BOMB

Bomb disposal robots are equipped with a wide range of devices to help them detect explosives and bombs. For example, they have microphones to listen out for ticking sounds and cameras that send real-time video images back to human operators. These cameras are often mounted on a robot's moving arm and can tilt and turn to give a full view of the surrounding area. Robots also have infrared cameras to see in the dark.

BOT SNIFFER DOGS?

Some bomb detection robots also have sensors that can "sniff out" explosives and bombs. They do this by detecting **vapors** that would be too faint for a human to smell. The inventors of these robotic sniffer dogs have created a library of smells for their robots to learn. Some robotic sniffer dogs can detect and measure odors, or smells, with a level of sensitivity usually only found in real animals.

Robots fitted with a long, jointed arm can lift and remove bombs so they can be disposed of safely.

X-RAY VISION

Some bomb detection bots also have portable X-ray machines. X-rays can pass through some solid objects—for example, X-rays travel through card and fabric but do not travel easily through metal. The Andros Wolverine robotic X-ray device allows the robot to see through a fabric, plastic, or cardboard object, such as a bag or box, to detect if there is a metal bomb hidden inside.

DRAG AND DUMP

Once a bomb has been located, a large disposal robot may be used to get rid of it. In this instance, the robot drives slowly up to the bomb, lifts it, and carries it away to a special container where it can be detonated, or exploded, safely and without damaging the surroundings. Sometimes, the bomb is detonated safely outdoors.

ROBOTS RISING UP!

Some bomb disposal bots are designed to disrupt a wide range of explosive devices using water. When activated, the robot rapidly injects a water jet at high speed. This is able to quickly separate key parts of an explosive device, making the bomb useless.

Robots used by bomb squads are kitted out with tools especially designed for bomb-disposal missions.

Sudden, unpredictable movements can explode a bomb, so it is much safer to send in a robot than a human officer.

BOMB BOTS ON THE BLOCK

Dragging away bombs and spraying them with water can work if a bomb is in an open area that's cleared of people and not too close to property. In more confined spaces, bomb disposal robots need to be much more sophisticated. The latest bots on the block have two robotic arms fitted with different tools, including fingers that are nimble enough to unzip a backpack, and can carefully defuse or disarm the bomb stored inside.

TWO-ARMED TACTICS

Having two arms is an advantage because the bots can use one arm to change the tools attached at the end of the other arm. This saves time as the robot doesn't have to return to an operator to do this. Also, the second arm can collect evidence at the scene to ensure that the person who left the explosive device can be tracked down later. Caliber MK4 has two independently operated arms with various attachments. It has a special, toughened hammer for breaking windows, and gripper tools for both arms so it can lift handles to open trunks or doors.

T7, THE ALMOST-HUMAN ROBOT

The T7 robotic control system pushes, pulls, and vibrates to imitate a feeling of touch. This is so realistic that the operator could easily believe they are working with human hands. T7 has one long, jointed arm that can swivel, or turn, in any direction. The arm can use pincers to grip and open or turn door handles. It can perform complex tasks such as unzipping a suitcase or unscrewing a cap on the end of a bomb container. The arm also has an extra-long attachment to help it access and inspect the underside of a vehicle. Another important feature of the T7 is that even though it moves on caterpillar tracks, it can climb stairs to get to bombs on upper storys.

ROBOTS RISING UP!

In the future, there will be more bomb disposal robots that can climb stairs and open doors and car trunks to disarm bombs. There may also be "throwbot" bomb-disposal squads. These are robots that can fling themselves over walls to reach otherwise impossible environments to detect and dispose of explosive devices.

Caliber MK4 can use its gripper attachments to open doors to reach hidden explosive devices.

ROBOT TAKEOVER: TAURUS VR

When the police are alerted to a bomb that has been left in a bag on the back seat of a car, they face a problem. Cars in tight parking spaces leave little room to get to the bomb. Most bomb bots are too big to help, so a human would need to risk their life to break into the car, unzip the bag, and try to disarm the explosive device inside. Not any more. The Taurus robot can do the job instead!

Robots Get Real!

The Taurus robot has cameras between its two arms. All a human operator has to do is strap on a **virtual reality (VR)** headset, and they can see exactly what the Taurus robot sees. Operators can monitor the information on the robot's dashboard and use controllers to move and control the robot, enabling the human bomb-disposal teams to get as close as they can to the action, without putting themselves in harm's way.

Controlling Taurus with a VR headset like this one gives a bomb disposal expert full command of the robot.

Taurus's robotic arms have plier-like pincers. These can pick up and use various tools, such as a screwdriver. They can even move a thin wire to disarm a bomb.

Taurus Takes on a Bomb

Taurus is lighter and smaller than many bomb bots. It can easily be transported and it can operate within confined spaces. As well as information gathered by sensors and fed through the robot's dashboard, Taurus's remote controls are fitted with haptic sensory feedback devices. Haptics mimic the human sense of touch by applying pressure, temperature, and vibration to the user, creating a sensation that feels real. It might vibrate to indicate warning signs, for example. Operators can even feel their way around a bomb.

BIG BOT DEBATE

Are Bomb Bots Life-Savers or Do They Endanger Lives?

Many people believe bomb bots have already saved lives and will take on more and more bomb-disposal duties in the future. Soon, robots will have the ability to detect and disarm bombs without the help of a human operator. Other people feel that putting robots in charge of bombs is dangerous and could actually endanger more lives. The robots could malfunction and use the bomb on a human. Do you believe that bomb bots are life-savers or do you think they make situations more dangerous?

Chapter 5

TRAFFIC COPS

Traffic police patrol highways, direct traffic, and deal with drivers and pedestrians who break traffic rules. They encourage people to be responsible when using public roads to keep everyone safe. From traffic robots that manage busy intersections to a robot that allows cops to make roadside stops without exiting squad cars, bots are already reducing the risk to traffic cops.

When the giant robotic traffic cops were introduced to the city of Lubumbashi in the DRC, there were fewer accidents on the intersections they policed.

GIANT ON THE ROADS

Highways in busy cities in the Democratic Republic of the Congo (DRC) in Africa are jam-packed. Pedestrians there are in danger because drivers often ignore traffic rules, even when traffic police are on patrol. However, it's difficult for motorists to ignore giant robotic traffic cops! Standing tall at 8.2 feet (2.5 m) high, these solar-powered robots have been successful in making motorists obey the law. They can move their arms to signal directions and they have changing lights to act as traffic lights. Their rotating chests also have cameras that beam videos of the traffic back to police stations.

ROBOTS RISING UP!

Some motorists respect and trust robotic traffic cops more than human ones. This could be because traffic cops in some places take money from drivers in return for not issuing fines and tickets. That makes it easy for road users who break the law to go unpunished. Some cops have even stopped innocent drivers and then made them hand over money before letting them go.

Drones can also be used to monitor traffic from above.

A TOWERING TRAFFIC ROBOT

Dressed in traditional traffic cop uniform, a traffic control robot towers above the highway on intersections in India. It can rotate, or turn, on its own **axis** to face the roads in different directions on a junction. It can also move its arms up and down to signal to drivers to stop or go. It has a set of traffic lights on its front that signal red, amber, and green to continually control the flow of traffic.

SPEAK UP!

Robotic traffic cops also monitor traffic using cameras to take photographs of drivers who do not follow the rules of the road. The robots have inbuilt loudspeakers that can be used to warn drivers or pedestrians that they are doing something wrong. These robots are proving to be successful, and officers have found that many more people have obeyed traffic signals since they were introduced.

ROAD PATROL ROBOT

Road patrol robots are motorized traffic cops that check that everyone is obeying the laws of the road. The three new traffic robots being used in Handan, China even look like traffic police officers because they wear yellow uniforms and white hats. They are equipped with automatic navigation so they can autonomously patrol the sidewalks. The main jobs of the road patrol robots are to identify drivers and take photos of anyone who is breaking traffic laws. They also look out for jaywalkers and warn them to stop. Jaywalking is when people cross a street at a place where it is not allowed or without taking care to avoid the traffic. It is dangerous, and it is illegal in some countries.

ON DUTY 24/7

Road patrol robots have sensors that help them move autonomously in every direction. They can take photos of cars that break parking rules, verify, or check, drivers' licenses, and direct traffic. The government plans to use the robots 24 hours a day, putting them in public locations including railroad stations and airports.

ACCIDENT AHEAD!

Another type of traffic robot is the accident-warning robot. It springs into action when there has been a traffic accident and human traffic police need to give instructions to warn passing drivers that the road ahead is busy or potentially dangerous. This frees up more human officers to do the urgent job of dealing with the fallout from the accident.

This road patrol robot can even give offenders warnings and take photos of incidents.

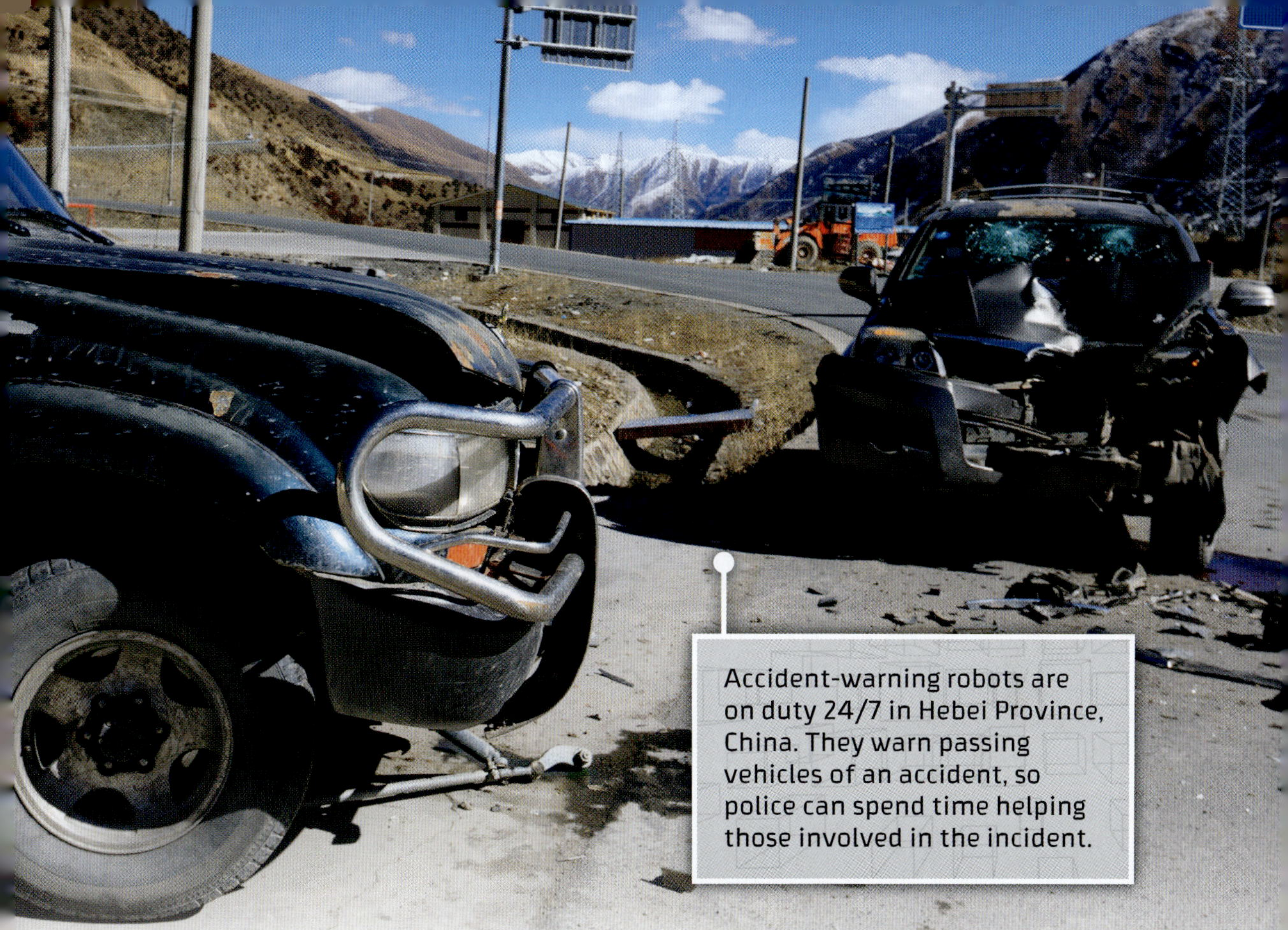

Accident-warning robots are on duty 24/7 in Hebei Province, China. They warn passing vehicles of an accident, so police can spend time helping those involved in the incident.

CAN I HELP YOU?

The traffic advice robot does exactly what its name suggests. People can ask it questions and it will answer them. These robots can provide drivers with traffic information and basic directions if they are lost. But, the robots also secretly scan drivers. Their computers can compare what they see with a database of people suspected of breaking traffic laws. If there is a match, the robots alert the police.

ROBOTS RISING UP!

In some cities in China, the highways are lined with surveillance cameras that people call "robocops." These are designed to identify the faces of badly behaved drivers and regulate traffic. At pedestrian crossings, anyone spotted jaywalking by the robocops receives an instant warning and a fine. Images and names of people crossing the road when the traffic lights are red and they should be stopped, are shown on screens.

ROBOT TAKEOVER:

ROBOTIC TRAFFIC COP IN ACTION

Every year, traffic police pull over many thousands of motorists. Most encounters result in just a fine. Unfortunately, there are also occasions when the officers or the drivers are hurt or even killed. To stop these outcomes, a police robot goes between drivers and officers to keep everyone safe. It's called the GoBetween.

Safety First

The GoBetween allows police officers to question motorists while both sides remain comfortable and safe in their vehicles. The robot maintains a safe distance between the officer and the driver, thus avoiding potential risk to both of them. For example, even if a driver becomes angry or aggressive, the robot won't do anything in return.

Protecting the Police

Using the robot also reduces the danger of police officers who pull over a vehicle, being struck by oncoming traffic while they are standing by the roadside. GoBetween makes it harder for the driver to get out of their car and try to attack the police officer or escape. It also prevents the vehicle from fleeing the scene of the incident.

How It Works

Once a traffic police officer has told a car to pull over, and parked their police car behind the motorist's vehicle, GoBetween rolls up to the driver's side window. A spike strip is automatically placed between the front and rear tires to prevent the motorist's vehicle from leaving the scene.

Traffic stops can turn deadly. Robots like GoBetween can keep drivers and cops safer.

In the future, more robots will be used at traffic stops to gather driver information.

Officer on Duty

Once in position, GoBetween becomes the traffic police officer's eyes, ears, and mouth. The robot shows the officer's face on a screen so they can communicate with the driver via web cameras. The motorist holds up their driver's license to the robot's scanner and their registration papers up to the camera for the officer to see. A small printer inside the robot can even issue the driver with a speeding fine!

BIG BOT DEBATE

Are Robotic Traffic Cops Good or Bad?

Some people say robotic traffic police are a good idea. They argue that the bots save human officers from potential dangers during routine traffic stops, and they keep citizens safe from the minority of police officers, who make mistakes. Others say that the bots are bad because they don't understand the human element in decision-making, for example, making an illegal stop because a dog crossed the road. Do you think robotic traffic cops are helpful or do you believe they will cause more problems?

Chapter 6

SPECIAL FORCES ROBOTS

Hostages are being held at gunpoint by terrorists. Armed suspects are holed-up in an armored building. A rioting crowd is on the warpath. These are just some of the dangerous situations that police officers may find themselves in. Sometimes, the risks are just too great to deal with and they need to call in the **special forces** of law enforcement.

WHAT'S SWAT?

SWAT stands for Special Weapons and Tactics. SWAT teams are **elite** groups of specialist police officers who are trained to deal with difficult, unusual, and dangerous situations and attacks. SWAT officers have high-grade weapons skills and wear protective armor, ready for a **firefight**. They use special tactics and machinery to get into and out of tight spots.

ROBOT SWATS

SWAT teams are always in great danger and that's why they call on a wide range of special forces robots to help complete their missions. These robots may knock down barricades, carry out surveillance, fire warning shots at the enemy, and more—anything to ensure a successful SWAT mission.

SWAT teams wear protective gear and carry shields, but they are still at risk.

INTELLIGENCE GATHERER

SWAT teams may literally throw their bots away! Throwbot XT is a rugged robot that is about the same weight as a football. It can be thrown in the same way too, easily surviving drops of 30 feet (9 m). As soon as it lands, Throwbot starts to show the SWAT force what's going on. It has an automatic infrared camera that can record and transmit audio, or sound, and video footage, even in the dark, from tens of feet away. The footage is sent wirelessly to a handheld controller. Its job is to locate armed suspects and hostages.

ROBOTS RISING UP!

Teams of three Throwbots can work together. They are each operated by handsets that transmit three different radio signals, so operators don't find themselves controlling the wrong Throwbot. The combined field of view of the several Throwbots can help give a SWAT team complete situational awareness. That means knowing what is hidden in a place and its exact whereabouts. This type of information is essential for planning a rescue or capture mission.

Throwbots can help SWAT teams locate suspects, confirm there are hostages being held, or relay information about the layout of a building to help the SWAT team plan its approach.

WARNING SHOTS

Bullets are flying, there is choking smoke, and loud explosions all around. A firefight is an absolute last resort on any mission, because it is a clear and present danger to everyone nearby. Some special forces robots fire warning shots to diffuse, or calm, situations well before any lethal weapons are used. They are a show of force and a way of warning criminals that if they do not turn themselves in, even greater force will be used.

LOOSE CANNON

Water can feel gentle on the skin but at high speed and under pressure, it can strike like a punch. Water cannons are special pumps with nozzles that blast out water in a particular direction. SWAT teams can guide robots, with water cannons fixed into position, to blast water as nonlethal warning shots. Water from a cannon can break up a crowd of rioters, or disarm a criminal. The water can knock over people and may cause bruising, but it is safer than bullets.

ASSAULT BOT

DOGO is an assault bot that is small enough to fit in a backpack. It uses nonlethal measures to decrease the tension in difficult situations. DOGO can quickly nip into the danger zone and feed video footage of the scene from its eight cameras to the SWAT team. The team can then control DOGO's actions.

Water cannons can be used as a nonviolent crowd control measure by law enforcement officers.

The DOGO robot can use a laser to pinpoint where suspects and targets are hiding.

CAUSING CONFUSION

DOGO's weaponry includes a dazzler, which produces a high-intensity flashing light and noise to distract targets up to 32 feet (10 m) away. It also carries a pepper spray that can fire half this distance. Once the enemy is disoriented, or confused, by the weaponry, the SWAT team can move in fast to make its arrests.

ROBOTS RISING UP!

Tactical UGVs (see page 14) face many tricky situations—but perhaps one of the more surprising is climbing stairs. DOGO has grippy caterpillar treads to help rumble over debris and bumpy ground, and pull it up stairs. To stop toppling backward at a steep angle, DOGO extends a rod from behind each tread. The rods act as temporary crutches to keep DOGO on track.

SEND IN THE HEAVIES!

The rioters own the streets —burning cars and pushed-over trailers are blocking routes, tire-bursting spikes are stretched across the highway. The SWAT team can't get close enough to clear the mob. If the team gets stuck, it would soon be under attack. It's time to send in the heavy bots to clear the way!

ROBODOZER

Automated robotic bulldozers are at the ready to clear the way in riots and other dangerous situations. They are not put off by the rain of stones and burning bottles from protesters and there is no driver inside that can be injured. ACER is a 2.2-ton (2 mt) powerhouse that is small enough to fit in the back of a pickup. It can then drive into the action.

ROBOTS RISING UP!

Robots are even taking part in hostage negotiations. Bots like the Mastiff have a 360-degree rotating and tilting camera unit on top and a two-way radio for communication between the SWAT team and captors or hostages. The system works like webcams that point in the direction of the person talking. Talking via a robot can make people less tense, so they can negotiate more easily.

Heavy-duty rescue robots can force rubble out of the way like a snow plow clears snow.

Equipped with a bulletproof shield and see-through panels, SWAT-Bot allows police forces to take control of hostile situations.

SLASHER BOT

ACER has a steel scoop to push obstacles out of the way. This can easily lift 1,000 pounds (454 kg). But if some debris is too heavy to shift, ACER's multi-tool can get to work. This combines a gripper and a diamond-tipped saw to slash through steel and reinforced, or strengthened, concrete.

SWAT-BOT

When there is no option but to face a hail of bullets, a SWAT team might hunker down behind a robot for protection. SWAT-Bot looks like a small tank with a bullet-proof shield the width of three soldiers but it can protect 12 people walking behind the bot.

BATTERING BOT

The shield is made from a special plastic that is much stronger than steel and is lightweight, yet it can stop bullets from high-powered rifles. A **battering ram** can be added to the front of SWAT-Bot. This is used to bash down doors, and bright lights can temporarily blind the enemy. Then the SWAT team can step out from behind SWAT-Bot and get to work.

ROBOT TAKEOVER: DIGIDOG

From inside their lair, the criminals see the backlit outline of a terrifying hound emerging from the smoke. But this is no ordinary law enforcement dog. It is the Spot robot, nicknamed Digidog!

Four-Legged Friend

Digidog is an agile bot with hinged legs that allow it to walk and run. Instead of paws, it has rubber feet. Its tall legs can help Digidog cover uneven ground more easily than small wheels. This 70-pound (32 kg) futuristic doggie can climb stairs with ease. It can sit, crouch, and stand tall, all controlled by an officer using a joystick at a safe distance.

Eyes in Its Chest

Digidog has no head. Its senses of vision and hearing are at the front of its chest. Here, there is a set of cameras lit up by regular and infrared light so Digidog can see in the dark. The rotating camera can zoom in to see targets far away, too.

This law enforcement dog can get close to the action without any risk of injury.